GUSTAV HOLST

FIRST SUITE IN E♭

FOR MILITARY BAND (1909)

Op.28 No.1
H.105

Revised Full Score based on the
autograph manuscript

Edited by Colin Matthews

Q.M.B. 501

DISTRIBUTED BY

CORPORATION
7777 W. BLUEMOUND RD. P.O. BOX 13819 MILWAUKEE, WI 53213

INTRODUCTION

In the notebook in which he kept a record of his compositions from 1895 until his death, Holst entered the '1st Suite for Military Band Op.28A'* on the page for 1909. This is the only evidence we have of the work's origins, for there is no certain record of any performance before 1920 (although parts seem to have been copied before 1918), nor is there any evidence of for whom the work was written. The same anomaly appears with the *Second Suite*, composed in 1911 but not performed until 1922. It is strange that these two masterpieces of band writing should not have entered the repertoire at once: there has certainly been no lack of performances in the years since 1920.

The *First Suite* was published in 1921 by Boosey & Co. in the form of a set of parts with a reduction for piano-conductor. A full score was not published until 1948, and this incorporated additional parts which had been added to make the work more suitable for American bands. It also included numerous misprints, since the score was compiled from the parts without reference to the original manuscript. Below is a comparison of the original manuscript scoring and that of the 1948 score.

Manuscript	**1948 Score**
Flute and Piccolo D♭	C Flute & Piccolo
2 Clarinets E♭ (2nd *ad lib*)	D♭ Flute & Piccolo
2 Oboes (*ad lib*)	Oboes
Solo Clarinet B♭	E♭ Clarinet
1st Clarinets B♭ ripieno	Solo-1st B♭ Clarinet
2nd Clarinets B♭	2nd B♭ Clarinet
3rd Clarinets B♭	3rd B♭ Clarinet
Alto Saxophone E♭ (*ad lib*)	E♭ Alto Clarinet
Tenor Saxophone B♭ (*ad lib*)	B♭ Bass Clarinet
Bass Clarinet B♭ (*ad lib*)	1st-2nd Bassoons
2 Bassoons (2nd *ad lib*)	E♭ Alto Saxophone
1st Cornets B♭	B♭ Tenor Saxophone
2nd Cornets B♭	E♭ Baritone Saxophone
2 Trumpets E♭ (*ad lib*)	B♭ Bass Saxophone
2 Trumpets B♭ (*ad lib*)	Contrabass Clarinet
2 Horns in F	1st B♭ Cornet
2 Horns in E♭ (*ad lib*)	2nd B♭ Cornet
Baritone in B♭ (*ad lib*)	B♭ Trumpets
2 Tenor Trombones (2nd *ad lib*)	Flugel Horns
Bass Trombone	1st-2nd E♭ Horns
Euphonium	3rd-4th E♭ Horns
Bombardons	1st-2nd Trombones
String Bass (*ad lib*)	3rd Trombone
Timpani (*ad lib*)	Euphonium
Bass Drum	Basses
Cymbals	Snare Drums
Side Drum	Bass Drums
Triangle	Timpani
Tambourine	Triangle
	Cymbals
	Tambourine

---

* He wrote '1st Suite' even though the Second was not composed for another two years; however the manuscript was originally entitled 'Suite in E♭'.

Since the composition of military bands and wind bands in general has changed since 1909, this new edition of the score does not attempt to go back wholly to the original manuscript (now in the British Library, London, Add. MS 47824). The second pair of trumpets and the baritone have been omitted entirely, while the added baritone and bass saxophones have been retained (with some emendations). The omission of the baritone has allowed the euphonium part to be expanded, most notably in the *Intermezzo* after letter D, and at the beginning of the Finale, where it doubles the 1st cornet at the lower octave.

Holst's concern to allow the work to be played by a small ensemble has been respected, and many parts remain *ad lib*. (It is possible for the *First Suite* to be played in this edition by as few as 19 players plus percussion). Particular care has been taken to 'cover' *ad lib*. parts. Since in the original manuscript all the trumpets were *ad lib*., the omission of the second pair has not left any serious gaps: indeed the opportunity has been taken to fill one or two that Holst himself left (in the Finale at Letter C, for example). Three cornets are essential, but the parts have been adjusted, since Holst, when writing for cornets in three parts tended to write for two second cornets (at the end of the first movement and the Finale the fourth cornet is optional). In the same way he was occasionally careless about the disposition of his four horn parts, and these are now organised so that the third and fourth may safely be omitted.

The only important places where an *ad lib*. instrument must be replaced by another are: the string bass, cued into the bass part at bar 16 of the *Chaconne*; the oboe, cued into the 2nd clarinet after letter C of the *Chaconne*; and the 2nd E♭ clarinet cued into the 1st clarinet for much of the *Intermezzo*.

Colin Matthews
London, 1984

The editor and publishers wish to acknowledge the invaluable assistance
received from Dr. Fred Fennell during the preparation of this edition.

INSTRUMENTATION

1 – Full Score	3 – 1st B♭ Cornet
8 – Concert Flute & Piccolo	3 – 2nd B♭ Cornet
2 – 1st & 2nd Oboe	3 – 1st B♭ Trumpet
2 – E♭ Clarinet	3 – 2nd B♭ Trumpet
4 – Solo B♭ Clarinet	2 – 1st Horn in F
4 – 1st B♭ Clarinet	2 – 2nd Horn in F
4 – 2nd B♭ Clarinet	2 – 3rd Horn in F
4 – 3rd B♭ Clarinet	2 – 4th Horn in F
2 – B♭ Bass Clarinet	2 – 1st Trombone
2 – 1st & 2nd Bassoon*	2 – 2nd Trombone
2 – E♭ Alto Saxophone	2 – 3rd Trombone
2 – B♭ Tenor Saxophone	2 – Euphonium
1 – E♭ Baritone Saxophone	2 – Baritone T.C.
1 – B♭ Bass Saxophone	4 – Bass
	1 – String Bass
	1 – Timpani
	4 – Percussion

Chaconne   –   1
Intermezzo –   16
March   –   32

Duration c. 10 minutes. The three movements should be played without a break.

* If there is only one bassoon, the player should take the second part unless a bass clarinet is
available, in which case the first bassoon part should be used.

BOOSEY & HAWKES Q.M.B. EDITION No.501

FIRST SUITE IN E♭
for Military Band

1. CHACONNE

GUSTAV HOLST
Op.28, No.1
revised and edited by
COLIN MATTHEWS

4

2. INTERMEZZO

*) play in the absence of string bass.

3. MARCH

35

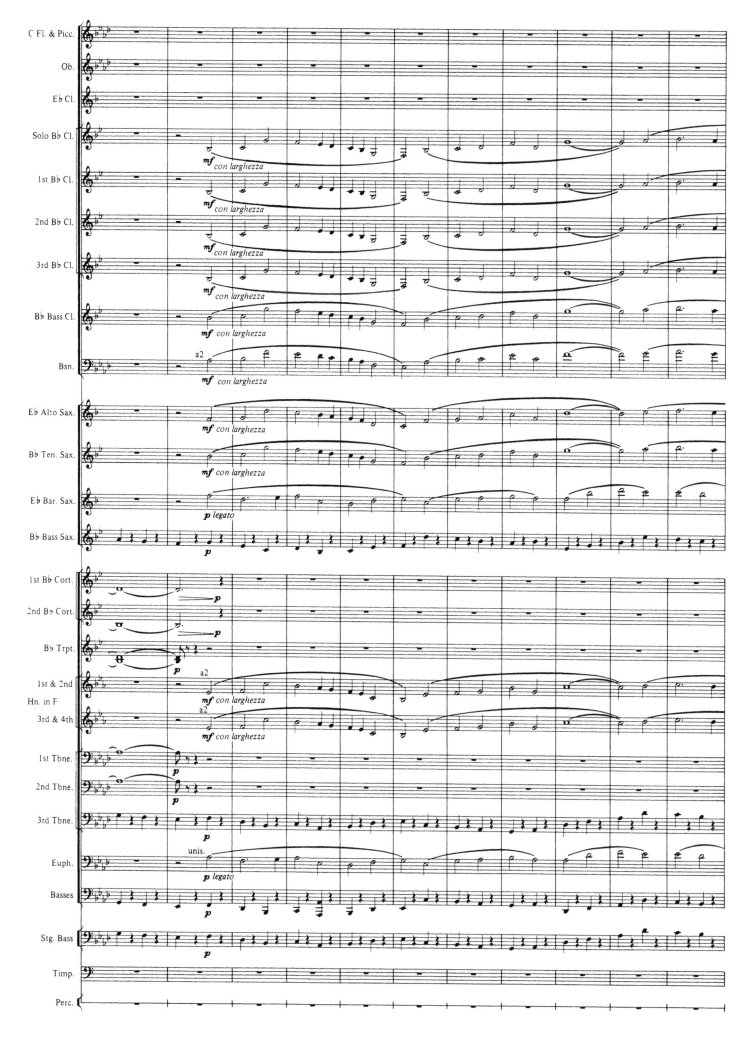

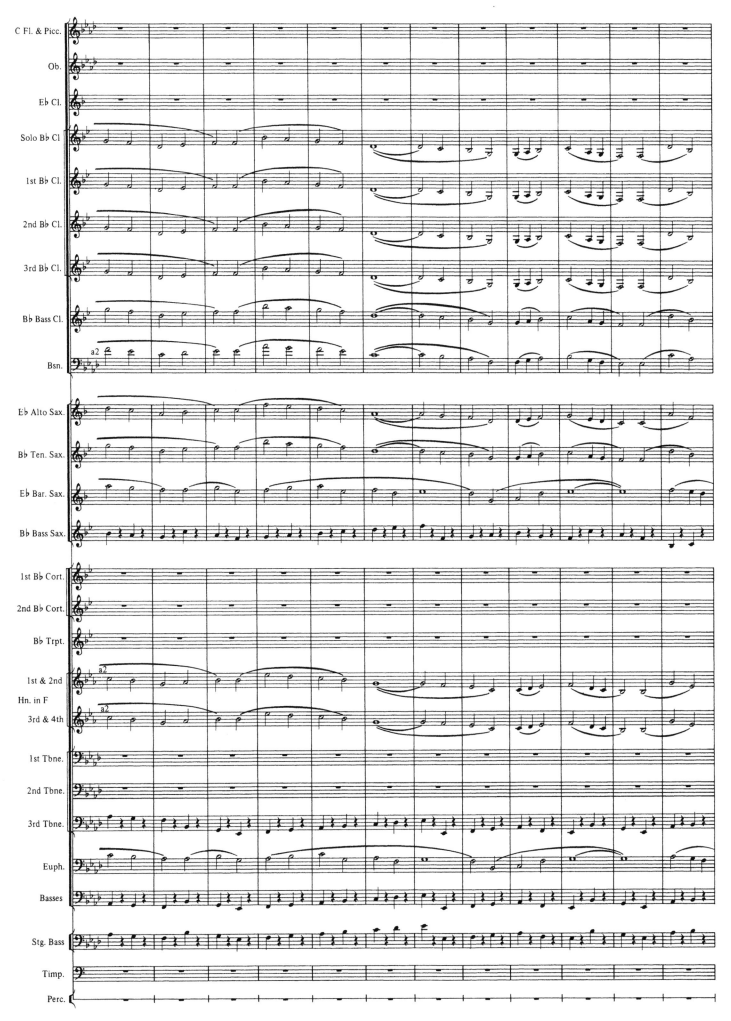

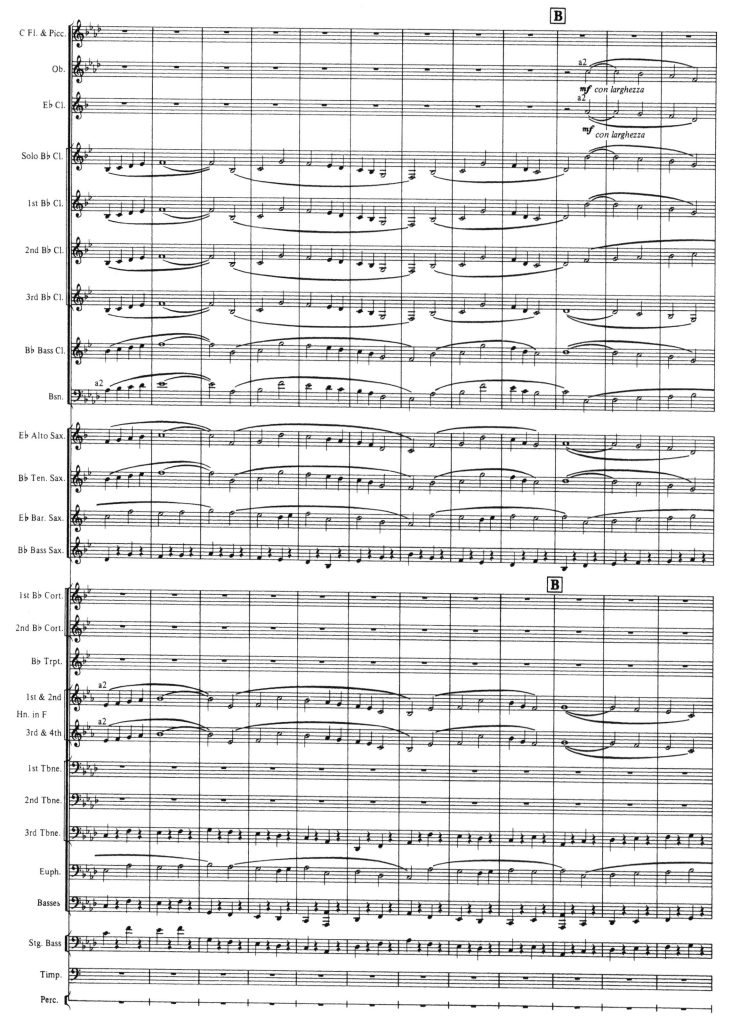

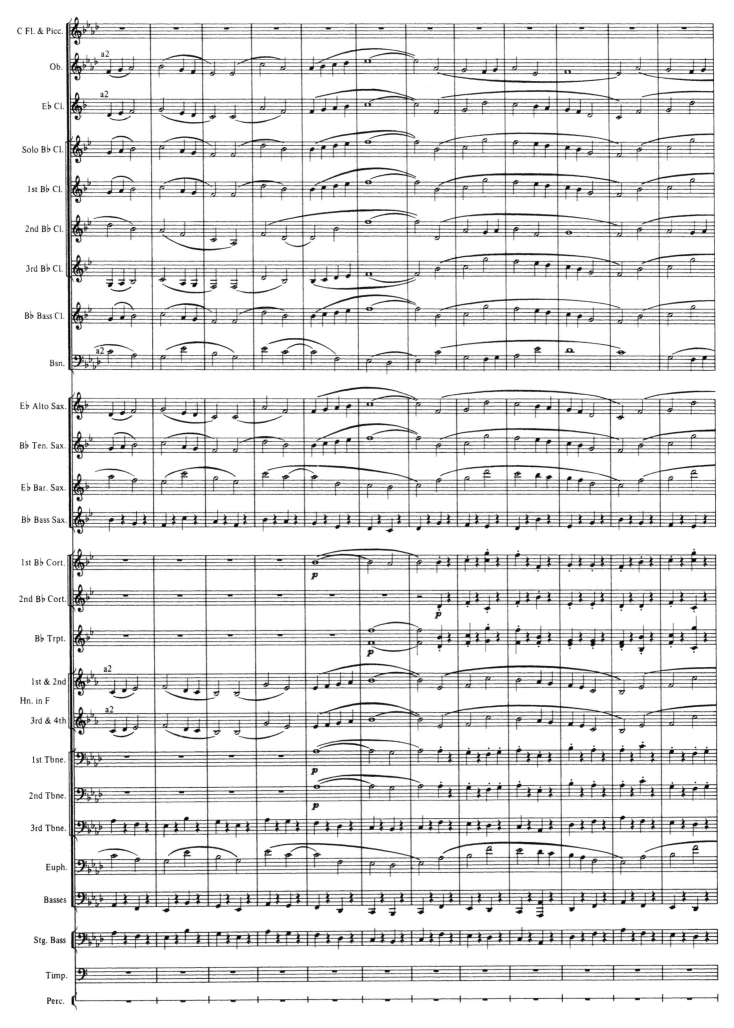

*) From here to the end extra side drums may be introduced *ad lib.*, all playing this part.

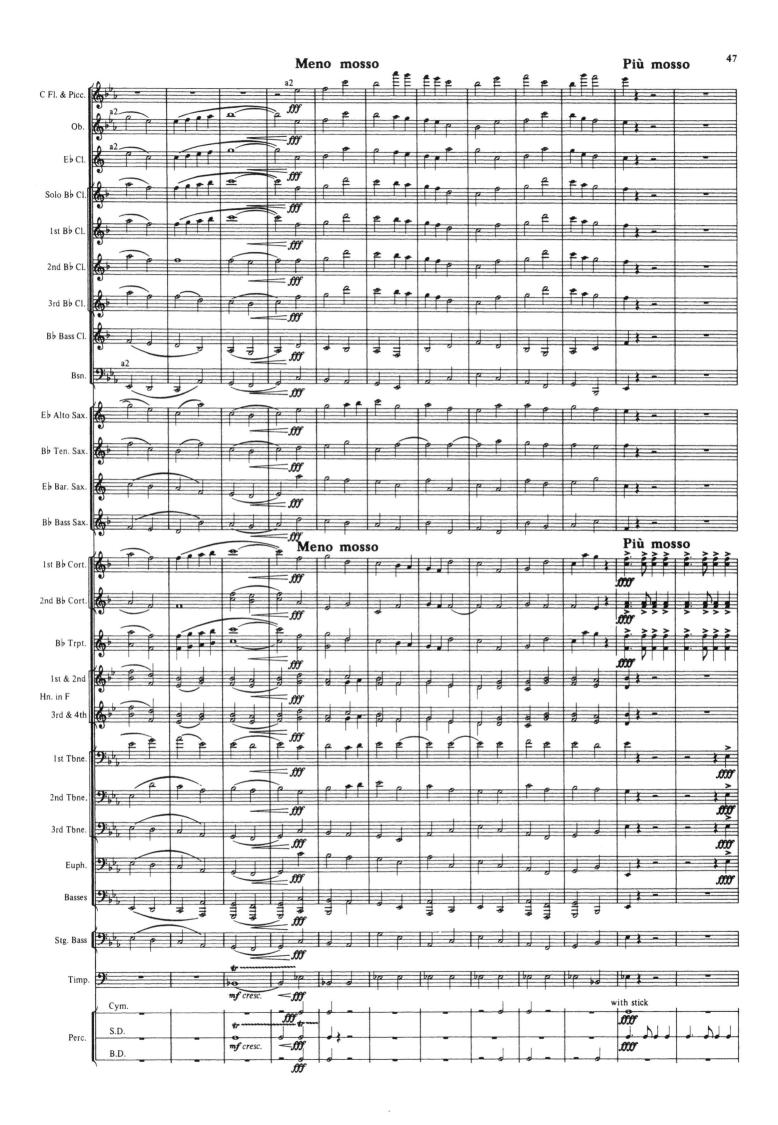

48

48010586

BOOSEY&HAWKES

DISTRIBUTED BY
Hal•Leonard
CORPORATION
7777 W. BLUEMOUND RD. P.O. BOX 13819 MILWAUKEE, WI 53213

M060052521

0 73999 75618 0